MW01242156

THE

LOVING

DISCIPLE

+ + +

*A Bible Study Based on the
Three New Testament Letters
of the Apostle John*

*by
Robert L. Tasler*

NOTICE OF RIGHTS

AUTHOR'S NOTE

The Bible references used in this work are from the English Standard Version, 2011 edition, an updating of the Revised Standard Version of 1971, published by Crossway Bibles. In this study the New Testament text is usually printed in italic. I thank my loving wife Carol for her proof reading and editing. Copies can be ordered at: http://www.bobtasler.com.

ALSO BY THE AUTHOR

(Paperback and E-Book)

Daily Walk With Jesus
Daily Word From Jesus
Day By Day With Jesus
From The Cradle To The Cross
Spreading The Word
Reflections
A Man's Devotions With God
Bobby Was A Farmer Boy
Fun And Games At Palm Creek
Palm Creek Pickles

(Bible Studies available in Paperback only)
The Hopeful Disciple *(1 & 2 Peter)*
The Called Disciple *(Matthew)*
The Practical Disciple *(James)*
Old Testament Disciples *(Major and Minor Prophets)*
The Obedient Disciple *(Philippians)*
The Faithful Disciple *(Colossians)*
The Loving Disciple *(1, 2 & 3 John)*

Table of Contents

Preface .... Page vi

Session 1 .... Page 1

Session 2 .... Page 5

Session 3 .... Page 9

Session 4 .... Page 13

Session 5 .... Page 17

Session 6 .... Page 21

Session 7 .... Page 25

Session 8 .... Page 29

Session 9 .... Page 33

Session 10 .... Page 37

Session 11 .... Page 41

Session 12 .... Page 45

Author .... Page 49

Preface to the Letters of St. John

DATE: The Three Letters of John were all written in Asia Minor around 87 A.D. by the same man, John the Apostle, youngest of Jesus' original twelve disciples. An approximate timeline of John's life is included after this Preface.

PURPOSE: 1st John was written to instruct the early church leaders how to deal with certain heretical teachers who taught that Jesus was not fully human or divine during His life on earth. They denied He was the Promised Messiah, but merely a superior teacher, the natural son of Joseph and Mary. At His baptism He assumed the "Heavenly Christ" symbolized by the dove, enabling Him to perform miracles. At His suffering and death, He assumed the "Earthly Christ" again, thus making the cross of little effect and the shed blood of Jesus not able to cleanse people of sin. In the letter, John shows love as a mark of the true believer.

In 2nd John the "elder" (John) writes to "the elect lady and her children" (Church and faithful believers), commending them for their faithfulness and also for resisting the heresy affecting other churches in Asia Minor at that time. He continues to emphasize showing love and to warn against traveling prophets who pervert the Gospel.

3rd John is written to Gaius, a loyal supporter of traveling evangelists who testified of Gaius' caring for them. Gaius is opposed by Diotrophes who was trying to control the church by refusing to welcome evangelists into the churches. In doing so, Diotrophes was opposing the elder (John) also.

Timeline of the Life of Apostle John
(All dates are best estimates)

6 AD   Born of Zebedee and Salome, possibly the sister of Mary the mother of Jesus

16   Lives in Bethsaida and works as a fisherman on the Sea of Galilee

27   Is called with his brother James to follow Jesus, and both are later called "sons of thunder"

30   Death and resurrection of Jesus, John is given the care of Jesus' mother Mary

40   Moves with Mary to Ephesus

48   Mary dies, John establishes churches in the area

55   Teaches many disciples, including Polycarp of Smyrna, a contemporary of Ignatius of Antioch

70   Jerusalem is destroyed by the Romans

81   Is exiled to Patmos by Emperor Domitian due to his influence among the churches

84   Writes the Gospel of John

87   Writes letters of 1, 2, 3 John

90   Writes Book of the Revelation

94   Is allowed to return from exile to Ephesus

98   Dies at age 92 of natural causes and is buried at Ephesus

Dedication

To Brian and Kersta as they pursue their loving discipleship in life together.

"The Loving Disciple"

A Study of the Three Letters of the Apostle John

Session #1
1 John 1:1-10

+ + +

1 ¹ *That which was from the beginning, which we have heard, which we have seen with our eyes, which we looked upon and have touched with our hands, concerning the word of life —* ² *the life was made manifest, and we have seen it, and testify to it and proclaim to you the eternal life, which was with the Father and was made manifest to us —* ³ *that which we have seen and heard we proclaim also to you, so that you too may have fellowship with us; and indeed our fellowship is with the Father and with his Son Jesus Christ.* ⁴ *And we are writing these things so that our joy may be complete.* ⁵ *This is the message we have heard from him and proclaim to you, that God is light, and in him is no darkness at all.* ⁶ *If we say we have fellowship with him while we walk in darkness, we lie and do not practice the truth.* ⁷ *But if we walk in the light, as he is in the light, we have fellowship with one another, and the blood of Jesus his Son cleanses us from all sin.* ⁸ *If we say we have no sin, we deceive ourselves, and the truth is not in us.* ⁹ *If we confess our sins, he is faithful and just to forgive us our sins and to cleanse us from all unrighteousness.* ¹⁰ *If we say we have not sinned, we make him a liar, and his word is not in us.*

+ + +

The Apostle begins this letter by telling his readers that what he writes is based on what he and others ("we") have experienced.

1. (1:1) *"...from the beginning..."* What beginning?

---

2. List the three senses (1:1) that John says show them of Jesus:

    a. _____

    b. _____

    c. _____

3. What does 1:2 say is the result of observing these senses?

    _____

4. What is *"the word of life"* (1:1)?

    _____

5. What is the purpose of this knowledge for the reader in 1:2?

    _____

6. What does 1:3 say is the result John wishes from the reader?

    _____

7. If they have fellowship with John, from whom will it come?

    _____

8. What does John say is his purpose in writing this (1:4)?

    _____

9. Who do you think John means by *"our"*?

    _____

10. Who do you think John means by *"him"* in 1:5?

    _____

11. What specific message does John give them in 1:5?

_____

_____

12. To what would *"light"* and *"darkness"* be referring?

_____

13. What does John mean in 1:6, *"have fellowship with him while we walk in darkness"*? How can Christians do that?

_____

_____

14. What did 1:6 mean by *"walk in darkness"*?

_____

15. What does 1:7 tell us about believers who *"walk in the light"*?

_____

16. What do you think it means to *"walk in the light"*?

_____

17. What is a result of *"fellowship"* mentioned in 1:7?

_____

18. Does 1:7-8 sound familiar? Where do we hear these words?

_____

19. How do we people today often *"deceive ourselves"*?

_____

20. What does John say will happen if we confess our sins?

_____

21. Why does John say God will forgive us our sins (1:9)?

_____

22. What are we doing if we do not believe we are sinners?

_____

23. How do you think people today feel about *"sin"*?

_____

24. How can Christians today speak about *"sin"* with others?

_____

Luther speaks about 1 John:

"The first epistle of John is a genuine apostolic epistle and ought to follow right after his Gospel. For as in the gospel he emphasizes faith, so here he opposes those who boast of faith without works. He teaches in many different ways that words are not absent where faith is... He does this, however, not by harping on the law, as the epistle of James does, but by stimulating us to love even as God has loved us."

+ + +

Lord God, thank You for giving us Your Holy Word. Help us to read it, learn it, believe it and live according to it. Amen.

"The Loving Disciple"

A Study of the Three Letters of the Apostle John

Session #2
1 John 2:1-11

+ + +

2 ¹ My little children, I am writing these things to you so that you may not sin. But if anyone does sin, we have an advocate with the Father, Jesus Christ the righteous. ² He is the propitiation for our sins, and not for ours only but also for the sins of the whole world. ³ And by this we know that we have come to know him, if we keep his commandments. ⁴ Whoever says "I know him" but does not keep his commandments is a liar, and the truth is not in him, ⁵ but whoever keeps his word, in him truly the love of God is perfected. By this we may know that we are in him: ⁶ whoever says he abides in him ought to walk in the same way in which he walked. ⁷ Beloved, I am writing you no new commandment, but an old commandment that you had from the beginning. The old commandment is the word that you have heard. ⁸ At the same time, it is a new commandment that I am writing to you, which is true in him and in you, because the darkness is passing away and the true light is already shining. ⁹ Whoever says he is in the light and hates his brother is still in darkness. ¹⁰ Whoever loves his brother abides in the light, and in him there is no cause for stumbling. ¹¹ But whoever hates his brother is in the darkness and walks in the darkness, and does not know where he is going, because the darkness has blinded his eyes.

+ + +

In the first session, we read that John wanted the early Church believers to understand how God has brought the light of Jesus Christ into a world filled with darkness caused by sin.

5

If they want to follow Christ, they, too, must walk in that Light, which will lead to fellowship with other believers. Sin keeps them from true fellowship, so they need to confess their sins in order to live in the light and fellowship of Christ.

Today's lesson tells us Jesus is the source of their forgiveness, and fellowship is not a new concept, but an old one given new meaning.

1. What is John's purpose in writing these things (2:1)?

   _____

2. Can you define briefly what the Law and Gospel are?

   Law:_____

   Gospel:_____

3. What words show the Law and Gospel in 2:1?

   Law:_____

   Gospel:_____

4. How is Jesus our *"advocate with the Father"*?

   _____

5. What is meant by *"propitiation"*? (2:2 – see dictionary)

   _____

6. How does Jesus forgive *"sins of the whole world"*?

   _____

7. How, then, does He also forgive each of us our personal sins?

   _____

8. How does 2:3 say we can show that *"know him"*?

    _____

9. What does John call those who don't keep His commandments?

    _____

10. In what way is 2:5 starting to sound like works righteousness?

    _____

11. What do you think is the purpose of John's words in 2:5-6?

    _____

12. What does John tell them in 2:7?

    _____

13. Seeing the following verses, what is that *"old commandment"*?

    _____

14. What other *"old commandment"* is often given with this one?

    _____

15. What do you think is the *"new commandment"* (2:8)?

    _____

16. How is the darkness passing away and the true light shining?

    _____

17. Who or what, then, is the "True Light"?

    _____

18. How does Matthew 5:43-44 compare with 1 John 2:10-11?

_____

19. In Matthew 5, Jesus is giving the old commandment a new meaning. Explain how John is doing the same in 2:7-8.

_____

_____

20. How might hate for a brother be *"cause for stumbling"* (2:10)?

_____

21. How does hatred show itself in acts of darkness today (2:11)?

_____

22. How does darkness blind our eyes?

_____

23. What evidences can we see today of darkness among people?

_____

_____

24. What can modern day disciples do about this?

_____

+ + +

Lord Jesus, help us fix our eyes on You for all things needful in life. Thank You for giving us hope for this life and the life to come, because You gave Your life for us all. Amen.

"The Loving Disciple"

A Study of the Three Letters of the Apostle John

Session #3
1 John 2:12-17

+ + +

2 ¹² *I am writing to you, little children, because your sins are forgiven for his name's sake.* ¹³ *I am writing to you, fathers, because you know him who is from the beginning. I am writing to you, young men, because you have overcome the evil one. I write to you, children, because you know the Father.* ¹⁴ *I write to you, fathers, because you know him who is from the beginning. I write to you, young men, because you are strong, and the word of God abides in you, and you have overcome the evil one.* ¹⁵ *Do not love the world or the things in the world. If anyone loves the world, the love of the Father is not in him.* ¹⁶ *For all that is in the world — the desires of the flesh and the desires of the eyes and pride of life — is not from the Father but is from the world.* ¹⁷ *And the world is passing away along with its desires, but whoever does the will of God abides forever.*

+ + +

In 2:12-14, John uses key terms identifying to whom he is writing. Most Bible scholars take the terms to mean three levels of spiritual maturity. Dr. Martin Franzmann (1907-1976), eminent Lutheran New Testament scholar, says "little children" refers to the church members as a whole, all those to whom John is writing his letter. "Fathers" are mature Christians, the backbone of the Church who know Jesus as the Word of Life (1:1).

"Young men" refers to the hope and future of the Church, those who have come to faith in Jesus and won the victory over the evil one during a time when such victory was very difficult. In repeated phrases, John brings home to them the unshakable certainties which are the basis of their love for God.

1. To whom is he speaking and why is he writing to them in 2:12?

   To Whom_____

   Why _____

2. To whom is he speaking and why is he writing them in 2:13a?

   To Whom_____

   Why _____

3. To whom is he speaking and why is he writing them in 2:13b?

   To Whom_____

   Why _____

4. To whom is he speaking and why is he writing them in 2:14a?

   To Whom_____

   Why _____

   _____

5. To whom is he speaking and why is he writing them in 2:14b?

   To Whom_____

   Why _____

   _____

6. Why do you think John repeats certain phrases to his readers?

    _____

7. What does John urge all three groups not to do in 2:15a?

    _____

    Why? _____

8. What does it mean *"to love the things in the world"*?

    _____

9. How can a disciple *"use"* them without *"loving"* them?

    _____

10. Does God approve of making money on Wall Street?

    _____

11. Give an example of each of the following from verse 16:

    *"Desires of the flesh"*_____

    *"Desires of the eyes"*_____

    *"Pride of life"*_____

12. How could each example in vs. 11 become a blessing?

    _____

13. Why does 2:17a say we should avoid things of the world?

    _____

14. What does 2:17b give as a reason to follow God's will?

    _____

15. What evidences do we see that the world is passing away?

_____

_____

16. How can Christians act or react to this *"passing away"*?

_____

17. The Holy Trinity is Father, Son and Holy Spirit. What might some people call the "Unholy Trinity"?

_____

_____

18. What is one way John's letter has shown us so far how to be a "Loving Disciple" (title)?

_____

19. In what way or ways can we fulfill John's words in 2:17b?

_____

_____

20. What one thing did you learn from this session?

_____

_____

+ + +

Lord Jesus, thank You for being our Savior. May we trust You for all we need to receive eternal life. Amen.

"The Loving Disciple"

A Study of the Three Letters of the Apostle John

Session #4
1 John 2:18-29

+ + +

2 18 *Children, it is the last hour, and as you have heard that antichrist is coming, so now many antichrists have come. Therefore we know that it is the last hour.* 19 *They went out from us, but they were not of us; for if they had been of us, they would have continued with us. But they went out, that it might become plain that they all are not of us.* 20 *But you have been anointed by the Holy One, and you all have knowledge.* 21 *I write to you, not because you do not know the truth, but because you know it, and because no lie is of the truth.* 22 *Who is the liar but he who denies that Jesus is the Christ? This is the antichrist, he who denies the Father and the Son.* 23 *No one who denies the Son has the Father. Whoever confesses the Son has the Father also.* 24 *Let what you heard from the beginning abide in you. If what you heard from the beginning abides in you, then you too will abide in the Son and in the Father.* 25 *And this is the promise that he made to us – eternal life.* 26 *I write these things to you about those who are trying to deceive you.* 27 *But the anointing that you received from him abides in you, and you have no need that anyone should teach you. But as his anointing teaches you about everything, and is true, and is no lie – just as it has taught you, abide in him.* 28 *And now, little children, abide in him, so that when he appears we may have confidence and not shrink from him in shame at his coming.* 29 *If you know that he is righteous, you may be sure that everyone who practices righteousness has been born of him.*

+ + +

John has said the world is passing away. He now gives them reason to believe his word; the Antichrist (one who is against Christ) is coming.

Living in the light (see 1:7) comes from having fellowship with other Christians. Living in darkness is from being deceived by His enemies.

1. To whom is John writing these words (2:18)?

   _____

2. What do you think John means by *"the last hour"*?

   _____

3. Whom do you think John means by *"They"* in 2:19?

   _____

4. What do you think John means by 2:19a?

   _____

5. From where does the Disciple's knowledge come (2:19b)?

   _____

6. What does 2:20 tell us we have and why do we have it?

   _____

7. Why does John say he is writing to them in 2:21?

   _____

8. What does John say is one mark of the Antichrist (2:22)?

   _____

9. How does John link God the Father and God the Son (2:23)?

_____

10. What is John urging of them in 2:24?

_____

11. What do you think it means to *"abide"* in God?

_____

12. What promise has God made when we *"abide"* in Him (2:25)?

_____

13. About whom is John concerned in 2:26?

_____

14. What *"anointing"* do you think John refers to in 2:27?

_____

15. What will this anointing do for them?

_____

16. To what *"teaching"* do you think John is referring?

_____

17. What does John urge them to do a second time (2:28)?

_____

18. Why do you think disciples need to be reminded so often?

_____

19. To what event is John referring in 2:28?

_____

20. What do you think John means by *"shrink from him in shame"*?

_____

21. What do you think is meant by *"righteous"* in 2:29a?

_____

22. What do you think is meant by *"born of Him"* in 2:29b?

_____

23. Note that these questions often ask "what do you think" in them. Why do you think those words are included?

_____

_____

24. What do you think are some qualities of a disciple?

_____

_____

25. Write one thing you have learned so far from this study.

_____

_____

+ + +

Lord God, save Your people from the evils all around us. Help us persevere and never give up believing in You. Amen.

"The Loving Disciple"

A Study of the Three Letters of the Apostle John

Session #5
1 John 3:1-10

+ + +

3 *¹ See what kind of love the Father has given to us, that we should be called children of God; and so we are. The reason why the world does not know us is that it did not know him. ² Beloved, we are God's children now, and what we will be has not yet appeared; but we know that when he appears we shall be like him, because we shall see him as he is. ³ And everyone who thus hopes in him purifies himself as he is pure. ⁴ Everyone who makes a practice of sinning also practices lawlessness; sin is lawlessness. ⁵ You know that he appeared in order to take away sins, and in him there is no sin. ⁶ No one who abides in him keeps on sinning; no one who keeps on sinning has either seen him or known him. ⁷ Little children, let no one deceive you. Whoever practices righteousness is righteous, as he is righteous. ⁸ Whoever makes a practice of sinning is of the devil, for the devil has been sinning from the beginning. The reason the Son of God appeared was to destroy the works of the devil. ⁹ No one born of God makes a practice of sinning, for God's seed abides in him, and he cannot keep on sinning because he has been born of God. ¹⁰ By this it is evident who are the children of God, and who are the children of the devil: whoever does not practice righteousness is not of God, nor is the one who does not love his brother.*

+ + +

John uses the word *"love"* 50 times in this brief letter, but in the first 2 chapters he has used it only 5 times. In chapters 3 and 4 he digs deeper into the meaning of love: God's love for us, our love for God, and our love for each other.

This love begins with the fact that God has made us His children. 1 John 3:1-10 speaks to all people of ancient and modern times as it contrasts the life of sin and the life of righteousness, which is living morally right according to God's standard of what is right and good.

1. What emotion or attitude does John seem to display in 3:1?

_____

2. Why does the world not know God's children?

_____

3. What does 3:2a tell us about our being God's children?

_____

_____

4. When will we know all about being God's children (3:2b)?

_____

5. What does our hope in Christ do for us (3:3)?

_____

6. What is *"sin"* according to 3:4?

_____

7. If sin is lawlessness, violation of the holy will of God, how does 3:5 tell us that God is serious about sin?

_____

8. If we are serious about abiding in Jesus, what will we do (3:6)?

   _____

9. What does John say of the one who keeps sinning (3:6b)?

   _____

10. What does *"let no one deceive you"* imply (3:7)?

    _____

11. What shows that a person is righteous (3:7b)?

    _____

12. What definition of righteousness was given in the introduction?

    _____

    _____

13. Whom does John say *"is of the devil"* in 3:8a?

    _____

14. What sinful behaviors have gained acceptance today?

    _____

    _____

15. What would John say if Christians approved of any of these?

    _____

16. Why did the Son of God appear according to 3:8b?

    _____

17. What do you think John means by *"God's seed"* in 3:9?

_____

18. What do you think it means to be *"born of God"* in 3:9?

_____

19. What result does being *"born of God"* bring in our lives (3:9b)?

_____

20. What do you think John means by *"keep on sinning"*?

_____

21. What shows whether we are *"children of God"* or *"children of the devil"* (3:10)?

_____

22. How important are our actions according to John?

_____

23. How do you think modern Christians display John's thinking?

_____

_____

24. What lesson does this give for today's Disciples?

_____

+ + +

Lord God, thank You for Your mercies that are new to us each day. In Jesus' name, help us to love and serve others. Amen.

"The Loving Disciple"

A Study of the Three Letters of the Apostle John

Session #6
1 John 3:11-18

+ + +

3 ¹¹ For this is the message that you have heard from the beginning, that we should love one another. ¹² We should not be like Cain, who was of the evil one and murdered his brother. And why did he murder him? Because his own deeds were evil and his brother's righteous. ¹³ Do not be surprised, brothers, that the world hates you. ¹⁴ We know that we have passed out of death into life, because we love the brothers. Whoever does not love abides in death. ¹⁵ Everyone who hates his brother is a murderer, and you know that no murderer has eternal life abiding in him. ¹⁶ By this we know love, that he laid down his life for us, and we ought to lay down our lives for the brothers. ¹⁷ But if anyone has the world's goods and sees his brother in need, yet closes his heart against him, how does God's love abide in him? ¹⁸ Little children, let us not love in word or talk but in deed and in truth.

+ + +

John now makes his central point of the letter. 1) To believe on the name of Jesus as God's Son and 2) to love one another as children of God, cannot be separated from each other.

Dr. Martin Franzmann writes: *"To hate, as Cain hated, is to be a murderer and a child of the devil and to abide in death. To love, as Christ loved, in word and deed, is to be a child of God, with a child's confidence before God, the assurance of being heard by Him."* (Concordia Bible With Notes, 1971, p. 496)

It is a test of one's faith to love others in deed and in truth, as Christ Himself did. To John, the commandment to love each other and to trust in Jesus as Lord and Savior are forever linked. It is a commandment that covers both faith and love.

1. What is the message they *"heard from the beginning"* (3:11)?

   _____

2. What does hatred make of Cain (3:12)?

   _____

3. What does it seem the devil always seeks to do to people?

   _____

4. What two things does John say of the devil in John 8:44?

   _____

   _____

5. Why should we not be surprised according to 1 John 3:13?

   _____

6. Give some modern examples of the world hating Christians:

   _____

   _____

7. Why do you think there is so much hatred in the world today?

   _____

8. Do you think there will ever be a world without hatred?

   _____

9. What does John mean, *"passed out of death into life"* (3:14)?

_____

10. What is the result of not loving our brothers?

_____

11. What does Jesus urge us to do in Matthew 5:44?

_____

12. How can we learn to love our enemy? What does this require?

_____

13. What does John call anyone who hates someone else (3:15)?

_____

14. What does John say a murderer shall not have?

_____

15. What does John say we should willingly do for others (3:16)?

_____

16. How does this echo Jesus in John 15:13?

_____

17. What does Jesus tell us to do in John 15:17?

_____

18. How do you think the apostle John got his ideas for 1 John?

_____

19. How does 1 John 3:17 compare with James 2:16-17?

_____

_____

20. What is John encouraging us to do in 1 John 3:18?

_____

_____

21. What things can we do to show love in our deeds?

_____

_____

_____

22. List some struggles a Christian may have being a disciple today.

_____

_____

_____

+ + +

Lord God, thank You for sending Jesus as our Lord and Savior. Grant us faith to hold fast to Your promise of eternal life through Him. Amen.

"The Loving Disciple"

A Study of the Three Letters of the Apostle John

Session #7
1 John 3:19-4:6

+ + +

3 ¹⁹ By this we shall know that we are of the truth and reassure our heart before him; ²⁰ for whenever our heart condemns us, God is greater than our heart, and he knows everything. ²¹ Beloved, if our heart does not condemn us, we have confidence before God; ²² and whatever we ask we receive from him, because we keep his commandments and do what pleases him. ²³ And this is his commandment, that we believe in the name of his Son Jesus Christ and love one another, just as he has commanded us. ²⁴ Whoever keeps his commandments abides in God, and God in him. And by this we know that he abides in us, by the Spirit whom he has given us. **4** ¹ Beloved, do not believe every spirit, but test the spirits to see whether they are from God, for many false prophets have gone out into the world. ² By this you know the Spirit of God: every spirit that confesses that Jesus Christ has come in the flesh is from God, ³ and every spirit that does not confess Jesus is not from God. This is the spirit of the antichrist, which you heard was coming and now is in the world already. ⁴ Little children, you are from God and have overcome them, for he who is in you is greater than he who is in the world. ⁵ They are from the world; therefore they speak from the world, and the world listens to them. ⁶ We are from God. Whoever knows God listens to us; whoever is not from God does not listen to us. By this we know the Spirit of truth and the spirit of error.

+ + +

Some commentators call 1 John 3:11-24, "The Test of Love," and 4:1-6, "The Test of True Belief."

The first part of this section, 3:19-24 ("Test of Love"), helps us know how to be sure we are truly loving as God wants us to love.

In the second part, 4:1-6 ("Test of True Belief"), John helps us know what it means to truly believe in Jesus. It draws a line between children of God and children of the world, between Christ and the Antichrist, between true prophecy and false prophecy. If a person believes *"Christ has come in the flesh"* (4:2), then that person is a child of God.

1. What is meant by "<u>this</u>" in 3:19, *"By <u>this</u> we shall know"*?

   _____

2. What *"truth"* (3:19) sets us free? See John 8:32.

   _____

3. If our sin condemns us, what can reassure us (3:20)?

   _____

4. If we aren't condemned by sin, what does God give us (3:21)?

   _____

5. 3:22 sounds like our prayers are answered because we obey God. Is this what this verse means?

   _____

6. What two things does Jesus want us to do in 3:23?

   a._____

   b._____

7. 3:20 states God knows everything. Is this always comforting?

_____

8. What is the result of keeping God's commandments (3:24)?

_____

9. How do we know if we *"abide in God"*?

_____

10. What do you think it means to *"abide in God"*? (see p. 15 #11)

_____

11. What opposes the *"Spirit of God"* (see 4:3)?

_____

12. What does John urge us to do in 4:1?

_____

13. How do you think we can do this?

_____

14. What else is coming into the world, even yet today?

_____

15. What shows us if a spirit is true or not (4:2)?

_____

16. What, then does 4:3a tell us of spirits?

_____

17. What is the indication that the antichrist is present (4:3b)?

_____

18. Can you see someone or something that is an antichrist today?

_____

_____

19. What does John say that should give us hope in 4:4a?

_____

20. Who in us is *"greater than he who is in the world"* (4:4b)?

_____

21. What should such knowledge do for Christians?

_____

22. Why does the world listen to the antichrists?

_____

23. What makes us different from them?

_____

24. Who does John say will listen to us and our message (4:6)?

_____

+ + +

Lord God, keep the Evil One from afflicting and affecting Your people and the Church. Help us trust in You for all things. Amen.

"The Loving Disciple"

A Study of the Three Letters of the Apostle John

Session #8
1 John 4:7-21

+ + +

4 *7 Beloved, let us love one another, for love is from God, and whoever loves has been born of God and knows God. 8 Anyone who does not love does not know God, because God is love. 9 In this the love of God was made manifest among us, that God sent his only Son into the world, so that we might live through him. 10 In this is love, not that we have loved God but that he loved us and sent his Son to be the propitiation for our sins. 11 Beloved, if God so loved us, we also ought to love one another. 12 No one has ever seen God; if we love one another, God abides in us and his love is perfected in us. 13 By this we know that we abide in him and he in us, because he has given us of his Spirit. 14 And we have seen and testify that the Father has sent his Son to be the Savior of the world. 15 Whoever confesses that Jesus is the Son of God, God abides in him, and he in God. 16 So we have come to know and to believe the love that God has for us. God is love, and whoever abides in love abides in God, and God abides in him. 17 By this is love perfected with us, so that we may have confidence for the day of judgment, because as he is so also are we in this world. 18 There is no fear in love, but perfect love casts out fear. For fear has to do with punishment, and whoever fears has not been perfected in love. 19 We love because he first loved us. 20 If anyone says, "I love God," and hates his brother, he is a liar; for he who does not love his brother whom he has seen cannot love God whom he has not seen. 21 And this commandment we have from him: whoever loves God must also love his brother.*

+ + +

The emphasis here, as throughout the letter, is on mutual love between people, especially in the church. Because some have left to follow false beliefs, there is danger of distrust and abandoning the love which is essential to hold them together. Their love, John says, will be tested, and so it is more important now than ever.

1 John 4:7-11 is probably the most well-known passage of this letter. Verses 7 and 8 have even been made into a short hymn in recent times, and verses 9-11 are the source of many, many sermons in the Church.

1. What is the source of love they can show each other (4:7a)?

_____

2. What does the ability to love show others (4:7b)?

_____

3. If we are unable to show love, what does it mean (4:8a)?

_____

4. What do you think 4:8b means?

_____

5. Does that verse mean God equals love? Why or why not?

_____

6. What does verse 9 say how we know what genuine love is?

_____

7. What is the purpose of that love according to verse 9?

_____

8. What does verse 10 tell us is the source of genuine love?

_____

9. Define *"propitiation"* (See 2:2).

_____

10. If God loves us, what should that cause among us (4:11)?

_____

11. Why does John say, *"No one has ever seen God"* (4:12)?

_____

12. If we love one another, what does it show (4:12)?

_____

13. What is *"this"* in verse 13 (2nd word)?

_____

14. What is the source of this love in 4:13b?

_____

15. What does *"we have seen and testify"* tell us (4:14)?

_____

_____

16. How did they know Jesus was God's Son and Savior?

_____

17. How can they know which persons truly believe in Jesus?

_____

18. Once again, what do you think *"abides in him"* means (4:16)?

_____

19. What will God's love give them in the day of judgment (4:17)?

_____

20. What will God's love do for them (4:18)?

_____

21. What do you think is the kind of *"fear"* John mentions?

_____

_____

22. How are we able to love others (4:19)?

_____

23. How does 4:20 connect with 4:12a?

_____

24. The purpose of 4:7-20 is summarized in 4:21. What is it?

_____

_____

+ + +

Lord God, thank You for Your merciful love in Jesus. Show us how we can love others as You have loved us, and then help us do it. Amen.

"The Loving Disciple"
A Study of the Three Letters of the Apostle John

Session #9
1 John 5:1-12

+ + +

5 *1 Everyone who believes that Jesus is the Christ has been born of God, and everyone who loves the Father loves whoever has been born of him. 2 By this we know that we love the children of God, when we love God and obey his commandments. 3 For this is the love of God, that we keep his commandments. And his commandments are not burdensome. 4 For everyone who has been born of God overcomes the world. And this is the victory that has overcome the world — our faith. 5 Who is it that overcomes the world except the one who believes that Jesus is the Son of God? 6 This is he who came by water and blood — Jesus Christ; not by the water only but by the water and the blood. And the Spirit is the one who testifies, because the Spirit is the truth. 7 For there are three that testify: 8 the Spirit and the water and the blood; and these three agree. 9 If we receive the testimony of men, the testimony of God is greater, for this is the testimony of God that he has borne concerning his Son. 10 Whoever believes in the Son of God has the testimony in himself. Whoever does not believe God has made him a liar, because he has not believed in the testimony that God has borne concerning his Son. 11 And this is the testimony, that God gave us eternal life, and this life is in his Son. 12 Whoever has the Son has life; whoever does not have the Son of God does not have life.*

+ + +

How can a person know for sure if he is a child of God? John gives three criteria: believe, love and obey. These verses re-state John's purpose: **BELIEVE** Jesus is the Christ, **LOVE** God and His people, and **OBEY** God's commandments.

John's first letter is written to show the overwhelming love of God in Jesus Christ and our need to reflect that love in our faith and life. John's words are as simple and practical as he can write them. It is his prayer that all who read them will also be as convinced of Jesus's Lordship as he is.

1. What does John say is a result of believing in Jesus (5:1)?

   _____

2. What do you think *"born of God"* means?

   _____

3. What is a result of loving the Father?

   _____

4. Why do you think loving God will help us love others?

   _____

5. What does 5:2 tell us is evidence that we love others?

   _____

6. What does 5:3a tell us is evidence that we love God?

   _____

7. How can God's commandments not be burdensome (5:3b)?

   _____

8. What does 5:4 tell us is a result of being born of God?

    _____

9. What overcomes the world?

    _____

10. Why or how can faith overcome the world (5:4)?

    _____

11. In whom is that faith centered (5:5)?

    _____

12. What do you think John means by *"overcome the world"*?

    _____

13. What do you think Jesus' *"water and blood"* signify?

    Water_____

    Blood_____

14. Why do you think John says both water and blood are needed?

    _____

15. When and how did the Spirit testify of Jesus (5:6)?

    When_____ How_____

16. What does John say is important about the Spirit's testifying?

    _____

17. On what do the Spirit, water and blood agree (5:8)?

    _____

35

18. What is the testimony of God greater than (5:9)?

_____

20. Why is that important?

_____

21. Where is the source of the testimony about Jesus (5:10)?

_____

22. According to 5:10, what would make person a liar?

_____

23. What is the testimony John wants his people to believe (5:11)?

_____

24. What does believing in that testimony give a person?

_____

25. How can we be sure we have this testimony?

_____

+ + +

Dear Lord Jesus, thank You for revealing Yourself to us through the Holy Spirit. Help us always to believe You are the Son of God and Savior of all. Amen.

"The Loving Disciple"

A Study of the Three Letters of the Apostle John

Session #10
1 John 5:13-21

+ + +

5 *13 I write these things to you who believe in the name of the Son of God that you may know that you have eternal life. 14 And this is the confidence that we have toward him, that if we ask anything according to his will he hears us. 15 And if we know that he hears us in whatever we ask, we know that we have the requests that we have asked of him. 16 If anyone sees his brother committing a sin not leading to death, he shall ask, and God will give him life – to those who commit sins that do not lead to death. There is sin that leads to death; I do not say that one should pray for that. 17 All wrongdoing is sin, but there is sin that does not lead to death. 18 We know that everyone who has been born of God does not keep on sinning, but he who was born of God protects him, and the evil one does not touch him. 19 We know that we are from God, and the whole world lies in the power of the evil one. 20 And we know that the Son of God has come and has given us understanding, so that we may know him who is true; and we are in him who is true, in his Son Jesus Christ. He is the true God and eternal life. 21 Little children, keep yourselves from idols.*

+ + +

The Apostle John concludes this letter, as he concluded his Gospel, with a statement of purpose. John 20:31 says, *"These are written so that you may believe that Jesus is the Christ, the Son of God, and that by believing you may have life in his name."* 1 John 5:13 is very similar: *"I write these things to you who believe in the name of the Son of God that you may know that you have eternal life."*

In 1 John 5:14-21, John adds a postscript, similar to what he also added in his Gospel. There it is, the entire chapter of John 21, with its emphasis on Jesus' instructions to His Disciples. Here the postscript is 1 John 5:14-21 which gives John's further instructions to avoid sinning and especially to avoid the sin that leads to death (5:16).

1. What does John say is his purpose for writing this letter (5:13)?

   _____

2. To whom is he writing it?

   _____

3. What confidence should the believer have (5:14)?

   _____

4. State 5:15 simply in your own words:

   _____

5. What is John promising in that verse?

   _____

6. In 5:16 what two kinds of sin does John say there are?

   _____

   _____

7. In 5:16a, who is sinning?

_____

8. What are some examples of such sins?

_____

_____

9. What do we call the prayers that we pray for someone else?

_____

10. What do you think is the kind of sin *"that leads to death"*?

_____

11. Why might John say they don't have to pray for that sin?

_____

12. How or for what should a Christian pray for unbelievers?

_____

13. In 5:17, how can John say some sin does not lead to death?

_____

_____

14. What understanding does 5:18 give to our answer in #13?

_____

_____

15. What gruesome fact does John state in 5:19b?

_____

16. Why should that not worry a believer according to 5:19a?

_____

17. Which group of Christians speaks of "venial" and "mortal" sins?

_____

18. How could one kind of sin be "mortal" and another not?

_____

19. What does Romans 3:23 tell us?

_____

20. What does 1 John 5:20 tell us is the purpose of Jesus' coming?

_____

_____

21. What does 5:20c affirm for us?

_____

22. What is worship of any other god than Jesus (5:21)?

_____

23. How could 5:21 be a concise summary of 1 John?

_____

_____

+ + +

Lord Jesus, help us trust You alone as our true God. Keep us from following any idol of this world. Amen.

"The Loving Disciple"
A Study of the Three Letters of the Apostle John

Session #11
2 John 1-11

+ + +

[1] *The elder to the elect lady and her children, whom I love in truth, and not only I, but also all who know the truth,* [2] *because of the truth that abides in us and will be with us forever:* [3] *Grace, mercy, and peace will be with us, from God the Father and from Jesus Christ the Father's Son, in truth and love.* [4] *I rejoiced greatly to find some of your children walking in the truth, just as we were commanded by the Father.* [5] *And now I ask you, dear lady – not as though I were writing you a new commandment, but the one we have had from the beginning – that we love one another.* [6] *And this is love, that we walk according to his commandments; this is the commandment, just as you have heard from the beginning, so that you should walk in it.* [7] *For many deceivers have gone out into the world, those who do not confess the coming of Jesus Christ in the flesh. Such a one is the deceiver and the antichrist.* [8] *Watch yourselves, so that you may not lose what we have worked for, but may win a full reward.* [9] *Everyone who goes on ahead and does not abide in the teaching of Christ, does not have God. Whoever abides in the teaching has both the Father and the Son.* [10] *If anyone comes to you and does not bring this teaching, do not receive him into your house or give him any greeting,* [11] *for whoever greets him takes part in his wicked works.*

+ + +

In this letter, the *"elder"* (the apostle John) speaks to the *"elect lady and her children"* (the Church and its faithful member. See p. vi) He commends them for their faithfulness and

41

resistance to the Gnostic heresy that is affecting many congregations in Asia Minor.

<u>The Gnostic Heresy Briefly Explained:</u>

1) <u>Matter</u> is evil, but spirit is good, therefore God is good.
2) <u>Salvation</u> is not through faith in Jesus, but from acquiring special knowledge (gnosis).
3) <u>Jesus</u> was not fully human, but only seemed human and a spiritual Christ lived as the human Christ on earth for awhile.
4) <u>Asceticism</u>: The body is evil, so we must abstain from all worldly pleasures. Materialism in life is reduced to simplicity but without maiming the body or making it suffer.
5) <u>Licentiousness</u>: Since matter is evil and salvation has nothing to do with the commandments, immorality can be allowed.
(Note how #4 and #5 conflict with each other)

1. What *"truth"* do you think John refers to? (See session 7, #2)

   _____

2. How many times is *"truth"* mentioned in 2 John?

   _____

3. How many times is *"truth"* mentioned in Session 12?

   _____

4. If *"truth"* is so emphasized, what does John want them to do?

   To_____

   And not _____

5. How long will the truth remain (v. 2)?

   _____

6. What three things does he wish for them from God (vs. 3)?

a._____

b._____

c._____

7. What fundamental truth does John tell them in vs.3b?

_____

8. What fundamental action does John ask of them in vs. 4?

_____

9. In vs. 6, how does John define love?

_____

10. Which Gnostic teaching is mentioned in vs. 7?

_____

11. What does John call one who teaches this?

_____

12. How would they lose what they have worked for (vs. 8)?

_____

13. *"Goes on ahead"* means for someone to rely on knowledge beyond the Gospel. What will that person lose?

_____

14. However, what will a person have if he abides in the truth?

_____

15. What does John caution against in vs. 10?

_____

16. What, then, is required of a Christian at that time?

_____

17. What do you think *"greeting"* a person meant at that time?

_____

18. What might *"greeting"* an evil person mean today?

_____

19. Read 1 Cor. 9:20-22. How might this conflict with 2 John 11?

_____

20. What is the difference between *"greeting"* in vss. 10-11 and Jesus' mingling with Tax collectors and sinners?

_____

21. What can we modern disciples learn from 2 John?

_____

Luther speaks on 2 & 3 John:

"The other two epistles of John are not doctrinal epistles, but examples of love and faith. They, too, have a true apostolic spirit."

+ + +

Thank You, Heavenly Father, for John's warning to remain faithful to the Gospel, and yet loving towards other people. Amen.

"The Loving Disciple"

A Study of the Three Letters of the Apostle John

Session #12
3 John 1-15

+ + +

[1] The elder to the beloved Gaius, whom I love in truth.
[2] Beloved, I pray that all may go well with you and that you may be in good health, as it goes well with your soul. [3] For I rejoiced greatly when the brothers came and testified to your truth, as indeed you are walking in the truth. [4] I have no greater joy than to hear that my children are walking in the truth. [5] Beloved, it is a faithful thing you do in all your efforts for these brothers, strangers as they are, [6] who testified to your love before the church. You will do well to send them on their journey in a manner worthy of God. [7] For they have gone out for the sake of the name, accepting nothing from the Gentiles. [8] Therefore we ought to support people like these, that we may be fellow workers for the truth. [9] I have written something to the church, but Diotrephes, who likes to put himself first, does not acknowledge our authority. [10] So if I come, I will bring up what he is doing, talking wicked nonsense against us. And not content with that, he refuses to welcome the brothers, and also stops those who want to and puts them out of the church. [11] Beloved, do not imitate evil but imitate good. Whoever does good is from God; whoever does evil has not seen God. [12] Demetrius has received a good testimony from everyone, and from the truth itself. We also add our testimony, and you know that our testimony is true. [13] I had much to write to you, but I would rather not write with pen and ink. [14] I hope to see you soon, and we will talk face to face. [15] Peace be to you. The friends greet you. Greet the friends, each by name.

+ + +

John's third letter is written to Gaius, a loyal supporter of traveling evangelists who is known for his caring for them. Gaius, however, is opposed by Diotrophes who was trying to control the church in Asia Minor by ordering others not to welcome evangelists into their churches. In opposing Gaius, Diotrophes was opposing John also.

This is the most personal letter of the three, less about instruction or doctrine and more about how to handle a congregational situation. It also has a more personal greeting and closing to the letter. John states he looks forward to visiting with Gaius in the near future.

1. By calling himself *"The elder"* what can we assume about John?

   _____

2. Once again John speaks of loving him *"in truth"*. How many times does John write the word *"truth"* in this letter?

   _____

3. What word does John use to show his feelings of Gaius (2)?

   _____

4. What does John write in vs. 2 that we might also write today?

   _____

5. What additional wish does John have that we might not write?

   _____

6. What made John rejoice in vs. 3?

   _____

7. What does John say gives him greatest joy in vs. 4?

_____

8. What does vs. 5 tell us about Gaius' activities?

_____

9. What is Gaius evidently doing for them (vs. 6)?

_____

10. What group of people is Gaius helping (see p. 45)?

_____

11. How does John feel about these people (vs. 8)?

_____

12. Who is creating a problem (vs. 9)?

_____

13. What does vs.10 say he is trying to do?

_____

14. What is John urging Gaius not to do about this man (vs. 11)?

_____

15. Why do you think the church usually has such a person in it?

_____

16. What would you say to Diotrophes?

_____

17. Whom does John recommend to help Gaius in this (vs. 12)?

_____

18. What does v. 13 tell us John wants to do?

_____

19. Why do you think John wants to speak with Gaius in person?

_____

20. How does John end this letter?

_____

21. Write two things you've learned about John from his letters.

a._____

b._____

22. What have you learned that might help you in your church?

a._____

b._____

+ + +

Thank You, Heavenly Father, for these letters from John that teach us about loving You and others Help us hold fast to the truth of the Gospel, and help us value and learn Your Holy Word all through our lives. Amen.

+ Thank You for your study of God's Word! +

Robert L. Tasler

Rev. Robert L. Tasler is a native of Windom, Minnesota, and a career pastor in the Lutheran Church-Missouri Synod, a conservative Lutheran body in fellowship with dozens of similar churches around the world. A 1971 ordained graduate of Concordia Seminary, St. Louis, Missouri, Pastor Bob has served parishes in North Dakota, California, Utah, Colorado and Arizona.

He and his wife Carol are retired and divide their time between Colorado and Arizona. They are parents of Brian and his wife Kersta, Denver business executives, and Chuck and his wife Debbie, Christian Day School Teachers in Phoenix, Arizona, as well as proud grandparents of five.

All the author's works can be seen and ordered at his website: http://www.bobtasler.com.

Made in the USA
Middletown, DE
11 May 2022